To stop water from seeping through to the next page, unfold the flap at the back of the book and place it under the page you're about to work on.

Dip the brush into water, then brush it across the black patterns within each shape to see the paint magically appear.

Usborne

Lunar New Year Magic Painting Book

Illustrated by
Bonnie Pang

Designed by
Alice Reese &
Catherine-Anne MacKinnon

福
吉
福
吉
福
福
福
安
福
福
吉
春

幸福平安
心想事成

春

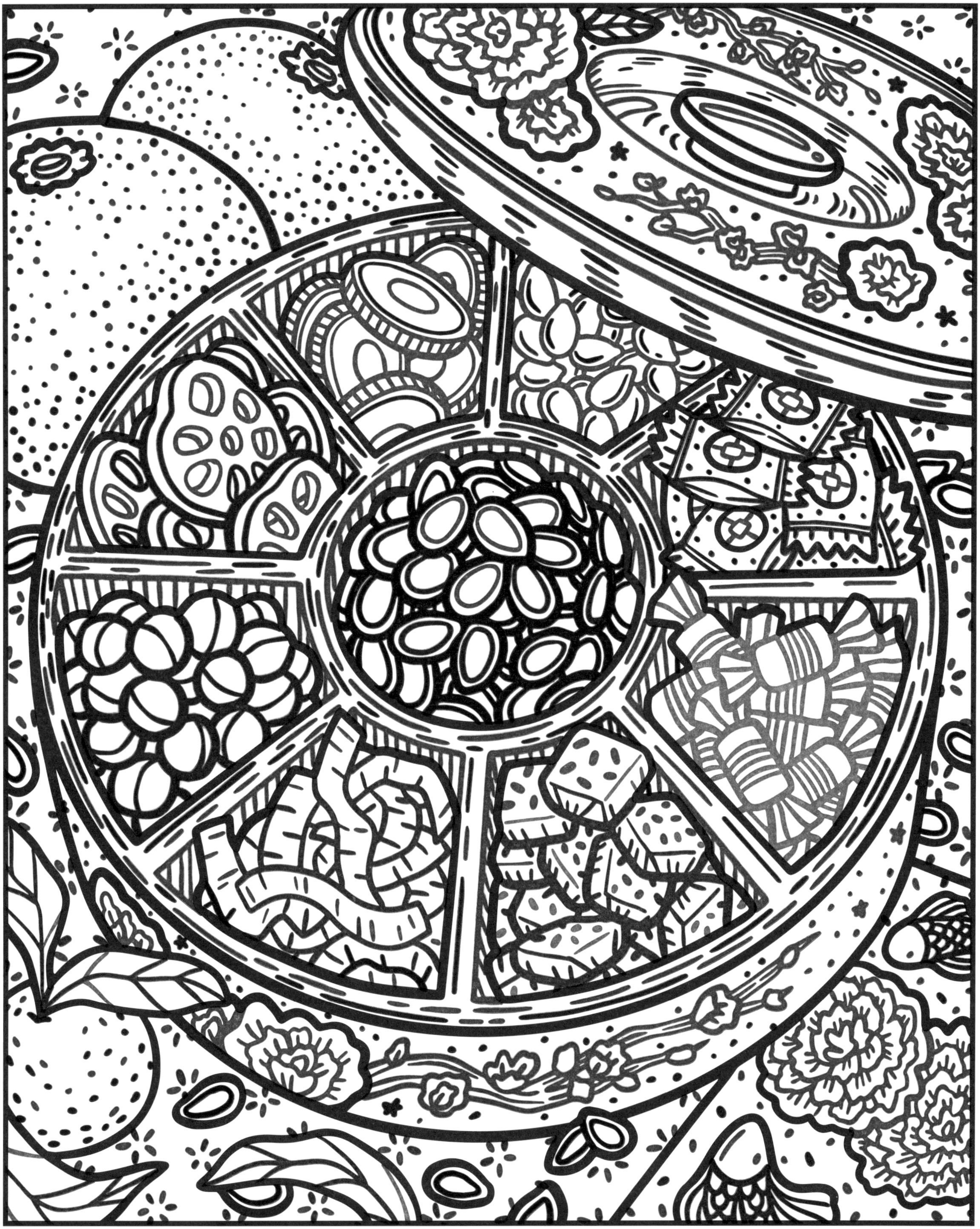